EXPLOSION OF CHICAGO'S BLACK STREET GANGS 1900 TO THE PRESENT

2/13-12   NBC

THE CHICAGO PUBLIC LIBRARY

CARL B. RODEN BRANCH
6079-83 NORTHWEST HIGHWAY
CHICAGO, ILLINOIS 60631

FORM 19

EXPLOSION OF CHICAGO'S BLACK STREET GANGS 1900 TO THE PRESENT

by Useni Eugene Perkins

Third World Press
Chicago

Copyright © 1987 by Useni Eugene Perkins

All rights reserved: No part of this book may be reproduced, stored in retrieval systems, or transmitted in any form, by any means, including mechanical, electronic, photocopying, recording or otherwise without prior written permission of the publisher.

First Edition
Second Printing: 1990

ISBN: 0-88378-120-4 (paper)

Manufactured in the United States of America

Third World Press • Chicago
7524 S. Cottage Grove Avenue
P.O. Box 730
Chicago, IL 60619

Production/Design - SERIF, Ltd.
Cover Art by Toussaint Perkins

Other Books by Useni Eugene Perkins

Sociology
Home Is A Dirty Street: Social Oppression of Black Children
Harvesting New Generations — The Positive Development of
  Black Youth

Poetry
An Apology To My African Brother
Silhouette
Black Is Beautiful
The West Wall
When You Grow Up
Midnight Blues In The Afternoon

TABLE OF CONTENTS

Preface 9

Introduction 11

Chapter One
EVOLUTION OF CHICAGO'S BLACK STREET GANGS:
1900 TO PRESENT 15

Chapter Two
DEFINITIONS AND THEORIES: THEIR APPLICATION
TO BLACK STREET GANGS 43

Chapter III
WHEN INSTITUTIONS FAIL, THE GANG WILL PREVAIL:
WHY GANGS HAVE APPEAL 54

Chapter Four
MYTHS, FACTS AND REALITIES ABOUT
BLACK STREET GANGS 61

Epilogue
A GENERATION NOT YET BLESSED 69

Appendix 73

The Author 80

PREFACE

This commentary is not intended to be a comprehensive analysis of Chicago's Black street gangs, nor does it purport to be based on scientific data. However, as one who has worked with and observed Black street gangs for over twenty-five years, I believe I do have some insight about them. Furthermore, I believe as a Black social practitioner my insight gives a perspective on Black street gangs that has not been provided by many white academicians and social scientists.

What this commentary attempts to do is to trace the evolution of Chicago's Black street gangs and identify those factors that have made many of them the violent gangs they are today. In doing so, I have tried to separate myth from fact and list critical realities we must face if we are to have a significant impact on Black street gangs. Although I do not provide solutions to the Black street gang problem, I believe some strategies for remedying the problem can be extrapolated from my commentary.

Useni Eugene Perkins
February 25, 1987

INTRODUCTION

Useni Perkins' book is long overdue. It is not 'a how to solve all of our black youth gang problems.' Nor is it the result of the current crisis in gang relations. Perkins writes from the perspective of a black insider to the gang phenomenon. Growing up on the southside during the 1940's and 50's and serving as executive director of The Better Boys Foundation on the westside, afforded Perkins insights only insiders can have. His earlier book, *Home is a Dirty Street: The Social Oppression of Black Youth* (Third World Press, Chicago, 1975) established him as a Black community scholar in touch with his people's deepest problems. This important work plus his numerous Black-impact plays identified Perkins as an intellectual who understood the negative effects of both institutional and systems racism upon oppressed black communities. Perkins discovered long ago the agonizing contradictions of being black in America—the same discovery which led Richard Wright to write *Native Son* and *Black Boy*; Ralph Ellison to write *Invisible Man*; and, James Baldwin to write *The Fire Next Time*. They discovered that the death of chattel slavery in 1863 and the subsequent trauma of the failure of Reconstruction (1866-77) gave birth to new forms of racial disfranchisement as thousands of rural blacks left the South for the urban North. Except for the NAACP, the Urban League, a few committed Black churches and Black colleges, the urban dislocation coupled with racial ghettoization and restrictive development, left the masses of urban blacks in cities without the economical and political foundations necessary to protect themselves from exploitation and manipulation by powerful forces. It is within this crucible that Black innercity gangs were born. The black youth gang is, therefore, an urban oppressed phenomenon whether in Chicago or Johannesburg, South Africa. This is one reason why Perkins' analysis begins with the 1900's. There is simply no understanding of the urban gang problem without this long-term historical perspective. From simple athletic bantering and rivalry ("if y'all win the game, you won't win the fight") to territorial defense against the racism of the earlier ethnic white gangs, the black urban gang evolved as a positive response to the seemingly defenseless position of many urban black communities. Many gang members who started out defending the black community have today turned into its greatest predators and destroyers. As Perkins indicates, because this is a crisis-oriented society, little was done about the hundreds of black youth destroyed through gang violence until all-American high school Basketball star Ben Wilson was killed in a senseless gang incident. The black community in Chicago and other major cities said, "enough is enough!" Perkins chronicles the evolution of violence in America with that of the growth of violence among black youth gangs and gangs in general. The gross and crass violence seen on tv, videos, movies and in magazines has ushered in a generation insensitive to pain and even death. There even appears to be gratification in the pain and death of others among youth today. When a youth sticks another youth up ("check it in" ... i.e., give it to me) with a gun the stickup gunman is just as likely to pump several bullets into his victim as not to. Kids are being killed for a pair of sneakers, jackets, earrings, gold chains, trousers and spending change. As Perkins indicates, if a kid wears his hat on the wrong side, crosses his arms or legs the wrong way, or laces his shoes the wrong way, he may be shot or beat up severely. The Symbolic Rights of Passage and Initiation of black gangs are almost unknown (as are gang territorial graffiti to most people outside the gang community) to most adults. Every black kid regardless of social class standing in the urban Black community is as acquainted with gang territorial markings and signs as he or she is with the names of the streets in the neighborhood! Survival depends on one knowing and respecting various gang signs and territorial requirements. When Perkins and I were youths many of our peers had to pay from twenty-five cents to a dollar a week to cross certain gang territories. Today they still pay. But, they may also be required to smuggle guns, contraband or even narcotics into the school environment. The urban youth gang is often an underworld subculture completely outside the particular community norms of most communities. Large gangs have been known to institute their own forms of marital and funeral rites! The fear and intimidation in which gangs use to control their territory and constituents forces many non-gang youth into arming themselves as a matter of self-defense. Those who join up with the mafia-type black gangs of today must adhere to a death-code. When it is violated the victim is killed according to a common ritual—as a warning to other potential violators The multiplying deaths from the growth of the mafia-type gang violence has caused some to view young urban black males as an endangered species. In fact, Dr. Benjamin Hooks, national director of the NAACP, predicts that by the year 2000 70% of the young black men ages 18-34 will either be in prison, dead or mentally ill. Perkins recognizes today's violence-prone gang as anti-community and anti-hero. The Harold Washingtons, Malcolm X's, Michael Jordans, Martin Luther King Jr's, Steve Biko's, Jesse Jacksons, Fred Hamptons, Walter Paytons, Sugar Ray Leonards, Lionel Richies are not their heroes. Pimps, con-men and hustlers who have $10,000 funerals—who are buried in gold cadillacs with thousand dollar bills in their hands—these are heroes to today's pathologically inclined gangs. Almost every institution has failed to effect positive changes in urban gangs: the school system, civil rights movements, police and Pan-African movements, criminal justice system, courts, prisons, churches, youth agencies, business community, politicians, welfare agency and sports organizations. Perkins has tried not to romanticize the destructive history of urban gangs. He has not glossed over the effects of slavery and racism upon the urban evolution of the black gang. Nor has he glossed over the Black community's failure to collectively grapple with this problem in its midst. Essentially, Perkins is calling the Black community to research and construct a new Black functional Value System which will provide positive belonging, identity, role models, security, discipline, support, parenting, self-esteem, love and communally shared experiences. As long as there are large cities, mass urban societies and familial breakdowns, there will be some forms of substitutes for people who feel powerless and dislocated. Where there is little or no sense of community or family, the gang often becomes a substitute community or family. Where Black men fail to organize, Black boys will run or ruin our communities. Where the Black community will struggle and gain control over its economical, political, educational, familial and religious institutions—and its cultural, athletic and artistic talent—there will be little need for negative substitute institutions. Perkins appears to be telling us that the entire nation of Black Americans will have to seriously modify and bring every institution into accountability if it is to redirect the fears, energies and aspirations of its young. Without such a redirection of values among Black Americans we might well evolve from explosion into urban gang holocaust in the late 1990's and early twenty-first century.

John R. Porter, Ph.D.
Chicago, Illinois
1987

I

EVOLUTION OF CHICAGO'S BLACK STREET GANGS: 1900 TO PRESENT

WHEN SEVENTEEN-YEAR-OLD BEN WILSON, A CONSENSUS all-American high school basketball player, was shot and killed a few blocks from the school he attended, the Black community was once again placed in a state of shock at what appeared to be another senseless and wanton street-gang killing. Although dozens of similar killings had preceded the shooting of Ben Wilson in 1984, none attracted as much media attention as did his untimely death. Immediately following the killing of Ben Wilson, community leaders, clergy and social service representatives began to echo their annual denunciation of Black street-gang violence. In previous years, their pleas routinely went unanswered and, in consequence, Black street gangs encountered little opposition. This time, however, due to the victim's identity and the passionate appeal of Ben Wilson's courageous mother, Ms. Mary Wilson, their voices aroused the concern of city government, the police and other public officials. There is something about the deaths of heroes in this society that provokes even the most apathetic individuals.

Ben Wilson's death did just that!

Although street gangs had been a menace to the Black community since the late fifties, seldom had the Black community reacted the way it did after Ben Wilson's death. Simply, the Black community gave notice it would no longer tolerate the abrasive conduct and violence exhibited by some members of Black street gangs. The resurgence of Black street gangs was now being met with strong opposition and renewed concern.

After witnessing Black street gangs literally hold some Black communities hostage during the sixties, the time had come to do something once and for all to abolish this urban abomination. But was this possible? Had the Black community allowed Black street gangs to develop to a position of indestructible power? Would it continue to see the lives of its youth destroyed before adulthood; have its homes marred by graffiti; have its businesses exploited by threats of extortion; and now become a war zone over the control and distribution of drugs? Had the Black street gang become so impregnated in the Black community that it would have to undergo an abortion to rid itself of this problem? These were some of the questions confronting the Black community in the wake of the re-emergence of Black street gangs in the eighties.

Prior to the death of Ben Wilson, there had been signs that mirrored the turbulent sixties when Black street gangs were at their peak. But these signs were ignored because there had been a lull in violent street gang activities during the seventies. This decline was largely due to the mass incarceration of key gang leaders which splintered the hierarchies of their respective groups. Although Black street gangs had not dissolved during the seventies, their activities were generally confined to random shootings or minor inter-group scrimmages. It is my contention that had the Black community mobilized sufficient resources during this period to reach those adolescents not yet committed to gang violence, today's gang problem would be less volatile. But, because Black street gangs were not raising the kind of hell they did in the sixties, the Black community was duped into believing the gang crisis was over. However, although street gang activity had subsided in the Black community, it had become increasingly active in the prisons.

During their confinement in prison, gang leaders continued to exert influence over their groups and began to use the prison environment to swell their ranks. Gang recruitment became a top priority and in some institutions, such as Statesville and Pontiac, gangs were being reorganized at a level of sophistication that dwarfed the types of structures they had developed in the streets. Perhaps this should have been anticipated in view of the fact the prison environment promotes group loyalty and conformity, both crucial components for street gang cohesiveness. Gang leaders took advantage of this opportunity and began to organize their groups to be more efficient once gang members were released and returned to the streets.

Release for many gang members came earlier than they had expected. Around 1980, the Illinois Department of Corrections (IDOC) initiated its now controversial early release program. The program was spurred by an increased prison population that had swollen to such proportions that some prisons were placing four inmates in a single cell. But, overcrowding was not the only reason the IDOC initiated its early release program. Many inmate advocacy programs were claiming they had programs that could help inmates re-adapt to community life, thereby relieving the state of its prison population problem and saving it money as well.

Once the early release program was in effect, hundreds of inmates were freed, and those with gang affiliations quickly resumed their gang activities. Since penal institutions rarely rehabilitate those they incarcerate, gang members returned to the streets as though they had only been on a sabbatical. Indeed, while in prison, many gang members developed a greater contempt for the law and also a greater propensity to violate it. Believing they had been betrayed by the Black community, many returned to the streets to exploit that community for their self interest. Now, however, after undergoing a major reorganization, Black street gangs were in a more advantageous position to achieve this notorious goal. The return to the streets of major Black gang leaders had an immediate ripple effect on the re-emergence of Black street gangs. The calm before the storm had now turned into a deepening resonance of uncontrollable chaos.

Although the fuse for this resurgence had been lit for some time, it was now ready to detonate an explosion that would shatter nearly every Black community in Chicago. Compared to the street gang violence of the sixties, the activities Black street gangs planned for the eighties were destined to be more violent and devastating. Gangs were now prepared to take control of the lucrative drug traffic and use it as a means to finance their criminal activities with complete disregard for human life. The flow of money generated from the sale of drugs enabled some gangs to legally purchase real estate and other enterprises. Profits from these activities were high, and there are estimates some Black street gangs have grossed over one million dollars in one year. Members of some gangs no longer wore the rugged style street attire of the sixties, but were seen in expensive three-piece business suits. Without question, gangs of the eighties had become more sophisticated, more enterprising, and more violent.

Many of the teenagers who comprised the gangs of the sixties had now become adults but continued to identify themselves as members of so-called youth organizations. This identification was grossly misleading because the Black street gangs of the eighties, as they were in the sixties, are controlled by adults. Granted, these groups do have large numbers of youth in their rank, but, nonetheless, their hierarchies are undeniably predominated by adult leadership. This phenomenon makes it difficult to differentiate between youth groups and adult groups. Consequently, Black street gangs are generally classified as youth groups, regardless of their adult influence and adult membership. The adults who control Black street gangs benefit from this misinterpretation because it projects an image that they are merely misguided and socially maligned youths instead of criminally-oriented, law-defying adults.

Since the mid-forties, Black street gangs had evolved from self-contained neighborhood groups, preoccupied with "gang banging," posturing, chauvinism, and committing minor felonies, to territorial monopolies, preoccupied with recruitment and expansion; extortions and killings; and the trafficking of drugs. The change was so dramatic that neither the Black community, law enforcement agencies nor traditional social service institutions were prepared to counteract their imminent danger. Despite the efforts of the aforementioned to suppress and/or quell their activities, Black street gangs continued to proliferate like a malignant tumor.

What brought about the re-emergence of the Black street gang and the explosion of its unharnessed fury on its own community? How did another generation of Black youth become so malicious and violent that many were willing to dishonor their parents and kill their own people? What happened to those cherished values which most Black youth once embraced, regardless of their economic or social status? What has contributed to the mentality of an oppressed people to cause them to vent their anger and rage on themselves? And, finally, is it possible to reverse these negative circumstances and re-establish a sense of order and sanity among our Black youth?

These are questions I have attempted to answer in tracing the evolution of Chicago's Black street gangs. In my efforts to achieve this task, I found little documentation on Black street gangs prior to the 1920's. While there exist numerous accounts of white street gangs roving the streets of Chicago as far back as the 1860's, this does not hold true for Black street gangs. One apparent explanation for this is that Blacks constituted a small segment of the city's population prior to 1900 and were not fully acclimated to the types of urban life styles and values which often foster anti-social behavior.

It is noteworthy that Blacks who lived in Chicago before 1930 were mostly second-generation southerners who still clung to those values and mores that governed the socialization of Black youth in the South. These values and mores were still binding on the behavior of Black youth and included obedience to parents; respect for elders; cooperative relationships; strong religious bonds; and a respect for the law. However, as increasing numbers of Blacks migrated to Chicago at the turn of the century, many of these values and mores began to slowly deteriorate. Apparently, the transition from rural to urban living placed demands and emotional strain on many Blacks which they were unprepared to handle. Coupled with the oppressed living conditions to which

Blacks were subjected, it is little wonder, then, that some Black youth eventually began to exhibit "anti-social" behavior. E. Franklin Frazier describes this transition as follows:

> The relation of juvenile delinquency to the organization of the Harlem Negro community is not so apparent as in Chicago, where, as we shall see, it is definitely related to the economic and cultural organization of the Negro community.
>
> In Chicago the percentage of Negro delinquent cases among the cases brought before the juvenile court has steadily increased since 1900. In that year 4.7 percent of all cases of boys before the court were Negro boys. The percentage of Negro boys increased for each five year period until it reached 21.7 in 1930.[1]

As more and more Blacks populated Chicago, there was an increase in delinquency among Black youth as well. This increase can be attributed, in part, to the high unemployment that left many Black youth with nothing constructive to do. Consequently, Black youth began to spend more time loitering on street corners and engaging in mischievous activities. As one might anticipate, these activities invariably led to Black youth hanging out together and forming cliques, major ingredients for the formation of street gangs.

But the formation of Black street gangs during this period was minimal, as evidenced by the Chicago Commission on Race Relations in its report that chronicled the violent Chicago race riot of 1919.

> Gangs whose activities figured so prominently in the riot were all white gangs, or "athletic clubs." Negro hoodlums do not appear to form organized gangs so readily. Judges of the Municipal Court said that there were no gang organizations among Negroes to compare with those found among young whites.[2]

Allan H. Spears draws a similar conclusion in his commentary on this infamous event.

> ...there were no organized Negro gangs—comparable to white "athletic clubs"—bent on furthering racial conflict...[3]

The few Black street gangs which did exist during the riot were organized primarily in response to the white gangs that were terrorizing the Black community. This distinction is important to note because it suggests that early Black street gangs did not pose a threat to the Black community but, rather, in many respects acted as guardians of their community. To retaliate against white street gangs that brazenly came into the Black community to terrorize its residents, Black youths were compelled to organize their own street gangs. This was a dramatic divergence from the exploitive and violent activities imposed on the Black community by the Black street gangs of today.

It was not until the mid-fifties that Black street gangs began to vent their frustration and perpetrate violence against the Black community. Prior to this period, the activities of most of the Black street gangs were confined to inter-group conflicts, misdemeanors, drinking and gambling. These gangs generally remained in their own neighborhoods (turf) and seldom ventured out into other neighborhoods except for minor rumbles with adversarial groups. The outcomes of these rumbles were usually short-lived and seldom involved the loss of life. Also, these gangs were generally comprised of close friends who attended the same school and participated in athletic and social activities. Seldom did they ban together specifically to engage in criminal acts. This does not imply, however, that individual members did not engage in such acts but, rather, that those acts were not group-conspired.

Athletics played an important role in the development of early Black street gangs. But the competitive nature of athletics was also a major factor in fueling conflicts between rival teams. This was especially true when one team would win an athletic contest on the loser's turf. Experiencing such a defeat before friends was an affront to a team's ego, and, often to compensate for it, the losing team would start a fight to save face. Such fights were quite common and although they were not full-scaled gang rumbles, they were frequently the catalyst for future, more violent gang conflicts.

Social workers have learned very little from these examples and continue to organize athletic contests between rival gangs. This was especially true in the sixties when detached workers or street workers attempted to use athletics as a means to buffer gang conflict. To their dismay, they painfully learned that athletic contests did little to foster inter-group harmony, and, as a result, spent a considerable amount of time policing the conduct of gang members during these misguided activities.

In his seminal study of Chicago street gangs, Frederick M. Thrasher disclosed that in 1927 Black street gangs constituted only 7.16 percent of the 1,313 gangs surveyed.

> A comparison of the percentages of gangs of [Negro] race and of white foreign and native extraction with the percentages of boys in these groups in Chicago shows that the gang is largely a phenomenon of the immigrant community...[4]

However, few of these Black gangs were violent or criminally-oriented, and as Thrasher observed:

> Many of these (Negro) groups are crap shooting gangs, and some of them, such as the "Bicycle Squad," engage in thievery.[5]

On the other hand, white gangs during this same period had notorious reputations, and were often involved in bootlegging, extortion and murder. These gangs were particularly prevalent among the Italians, Irish and Poles and, no doubt, served as "feeder groups," to Chicago's well-oriented crime syndicate. Some white groups controlled the political interest in their communities and were catalysts for spawning the careers of many white judges, politicians and businessmen. In his book on the late Mayor Richard J. Daley, Mike Royko cites the Hamburg social and Athletic Club, which once counted Daley as a member, as one such group. Located in the Bridgeport community, the Hamburg Social and Athletic Club was also cited by the Illinois Commission on Human Rights as having played a dominant role in the 1919 Chicago race riot.

Conversely, Black street gangs had no such influence and were not noticeably involved in the political and economic development of the Black community. Had they done so, it is conceivable that the Black community could have developed a stronger, more self-contained political base before the emergence of our first Black mayor. This is suggested in light of the fact most viable political movements spring from a common source and are nurtured over a period of many years. If early Black gangs had been politicized to use their power and numbers—regardless how small—to develop and support political candidates that represented the real needs of the Black community, my thesis may not appear to sound like a pipe dream.

During the sixties, there were a few attempts to seriously politicize Black gangs, if not around a political base then around a political ideology. The former was true of some community-based organizations, while the latter was advocated by various "revolution-focused" groups.

The political potential of Black street gangs first became evident during Chicago's Freedom Movement in 1964. Gang members were encouraged to participate in rallies, act as marshalls during demonstrations and take part in civil rights discussions. Leaders of the movement felt that this involvement would help it show greater strength and give gang members an opportunity to improve their civic image. But this move was not without criticism. Some people felt that the gangs were only using the movement to put them in a negotiable position with community organizations to secure jobs for members. Conversely, community organizations which used gangs were accused of exploiting gang members only as a tool to further their own bases of power. Both accusations were probably correct, but vested interests always have a priority when goals depend upon reciprocal relationships.

At one time, the Black Panther Party was making some efforts to politicize street gangs to become involved in constructive community activities. However, this was during the period when the Black Panther Party was engaged in constant confrontations with the police and its own image was being challenged as a subversive and violent organization. Also, many street gangs resisted these efforts because they felt that the Black Panther Party was infringing on their territories and would divert members from their groups. When the climate for an allegiance between street gangs and the Black Panther Party became favorable, the police had clamped down so hard on these groups that a coalition was not possible. Some people felt that the police realized the potential of such a coalition and made every effort to abort its formation. It has also been speculated that the police executions of Fred Hampton, Chairman of the Chicago Black Panther Party, and Mark Clark, Chairman of the Illinois Black Panther Party, were linked with this crackdown. Before his death, Chairman Hampton had been making some progress in mobilizing gang leaders around political issues.

Prior to 1930 there is little documentation to suggest that Black street gangs were either numerous or posed a serious problem to the Black community. In their definitive study of Black life in Chicago during this period, St. Clair Drake and Horace Cayton made the following statement:

> In 1930, 20 out of every hundred boys hailed before the juvenile court were colored boys. The rates for girls were almost as high. The Depression made a chronic condition acute. Parents were without money to give children for the shows, the dances, and the "zoot suits" which lower-class adolescent status required. There were few odd jobs. Purse snatching became general in lower-class areas and even on main thoroughfares. Occasionally, too, a gang of youngsters would crowd some other child who had a little money into a doorway and rob him at knife point. Studies of delinquents show that their behavior is partly "rational" (i.e., partly the search for a thrill of excitement).[6]

Drake and Cayton called these delinquents "wild children" and although their study did not go into an analysis of Black street gangs, they do provide us with documentation as to how Black youth were impacting the Black community. As competent, well-trained social scientists, we can reasonably assume that they would have documented it in their study had Black street gangs been prominent during this period. Since Drake and Cayton did not elaborate on Black street gangs, we can also assume that they were not a major problem in the thirties. This is, indeed, contrary to the thinking of many Blacks that Black street gangs have always posed a threat to the Black community. This perception probably derives from the tremendous impact Black street gangs have had on the Black community since the sixties. At times this impact has been so overwhelming that it is understandable why we sometimes feel that Black street gangs have always been entrenched in the black community. This is far from the truth—even though numerous studies have been slanted to lead us to believe otherwise. Perhaps when the Black community understands this distortion, it can begin to regain faith in its ability to restore those traditions which helped to shape the socialization of Black youth prior to the forties.

In the light of the documentation reviewed, we can with some confidence conclude that the impact of Black street gangs on the Black community was minimal, at best, prior to the 1940s. Even though thousands of Black youth and young adults were jobless during the Great depression years, gang activity among them did not show an appreciable increase. This observation, however, does not negate the fact that individual criminal acts by Black youth may have escalated during these depressed years. Nonetheless, they were not gang-oriented or gang-conspired.

During the latter stages of the Great Depression, a few prominent Black street gangs did emerge as exceptions to the rule. Perhaps the most noted of these groups was the Four Corners. The Four Corners was a group of young men who hung around the corners of 35th Street and Indiana Avenue, which was then known as the "bucket of blood." As a youth, I grew up near this area, and can recall countless stories describing the many exploits of the Four Corners. Although the Four Corners was not a street gang in the same sense that we know of street gangs today, it did perceive the ruling of turf as a measurement of its influence and power. However, the Four Corners rarely flaunted its power on the general public, and seemed content being recognized as a power broker for various criminal activities.

While the Four Corners reigned on the Southside, there was a noticeable increase of Black street gangs on the Westside. This was particularly true in the overcrowded, commercial district around 12th Street and Halsted, commonly known as "Jew Town." This district had been the hub of street gang activity for many decades and was the turf for numerous white ethnic gangs. Most of these gangs were organized as athletic clubs and operated out of storefronts, many of which still exist today. As Blacks settled in large numbers on the Westside, Black youth began to emulate their white counterparts. This emulation was not always of their own choosing, but often as a means of protection from the abuse of white gangs. Although many of these gangs did engage in criminal activities, most of their energy was expended fighting each other. Some of the Black street gangs were named the "Coons," "Dirty Sheiks" and "Wailing Shebas." These groups were the forerunners for the "Imperial Chaplins" and "Clovers" who later influenced the emergence of the "Vice Lords" and "Egyptian Cobras."

The names used by these groups were, indeed, interesting and ranged from the ludicrous to the paradoxical. For example, the dirty Sheiks and Vice Lords denoted royalty that had been corrupted, and the Imperial Chaplins conveyed an image that is highly religious, hardly indicative of the gang's activities. Other names such as the Apaches and El Commandoes could have been taken from the movies, while the Clovers came from a singing group that bore the same name. No doubt all of these names were given considerable thought at their origin and contain messages which we have still yet to decipher.

In addition to having controversial names, early Black street gangs took great pride in showcasing their gang symbols and colors by wearing colorful jackets and sweaters. This attire were proudly displayed and worn by gang members with little concern or fear of police reprisal. This unconcern was attributed to gang members' belief that they did not comprise a criminally-oriented group, and, therefore, should not shield their image from the community or police. This belief has typified Black street gangs and was evident in the 60s when berets became the most conspicuous symbol for identifying a gang's identity. In the 80s, these symbols have changed to a variety of idiosyncrasies, ranging from tying shoe laces a special way and hand signals to the way one wears his hat. Some groups, however, that allege to have religious affiliations, wear attire that is not intended to be deceptive.

By the early 1940s most Black communities, except for the so-called affluent ones, were exposed to some gang activity. Ironically, this activity continued to increase during World War II. While Black men were being drafted to fight the Germans and Japanese, Black street gangs were being organized to fight each other. After World War II, Black street gangs continued to expand and a wave of potentially violent youth began to emerge in large numbers. It was probably during this period that the passion of turf took on a greater significance and became crucial to a gang's identity and power base.

One group that received considerable notoriety around this period was the Deacons. The Deacons was largely a product of the Ida B. Wells Housing Project, one of the first public housing projects, located between 37th and 39th streets between South Parkway (now King Drive) and Cottage Grove Avenue. For many Blacks, living in this newly-built housing development was a blessing. It provided them, for the first time, decent living accommodations and a well-kept environment. With such accommodations, one would hardly think that the Ida B. Wells Project would be a breeder of street gangs. Yet, within a few years after the completion of Ida B. Wells, the Deacons were organized.

There are varied accounts of how this group actually got started. One account is that the youth who lived in Ida B. Wells were considered to be privileged and were resented by the youth who lived outside the project before the development of Ida B.

Wells, Madden Park, a neighborhood playground with a gymnasium and swimming pool, was where many youth in the community spent their leisure time. However, Ida B. Wells was built around Madden Park and it was felt by those who lived in Ida B. Wells that the park was their exclusively for their use and enjoyment. Of course, these feelings aroused animosity from the youth who did not live in Ida B. Wells, and disputes over who should have access to the park led to many fights and eventually inter-group conflicts.

Another account of how the Deacons was formed is that the nucleus for this group was organized before Ida B. Wells was built. And, as Ida B. Wells became populated with youth from other communities, the Deacons saw this as an opportunity to expand its ranks. There is more than a grain of truth to this because the leader of the Deacons, as well as other members, never did live in Ida B. Wells. Regardless of which account is actually true, the control of Madden Park was the catalyst that ignited the Deacons to become one of the largest street gangs in the Black community during the forties.

The hierarchy of the Deacons consisted of a president, vice president, treasurer and war counselor. The Deacons held regular meetings and maintained a tight bond between members. Most of the Deacons were in their late teens, and there was no forced recruitment of members. A complement to the Deacons was the Deaconettes, a group of young ladies. The Deaconettes were not just girl friends of the Deacons, but had their own hierarchy and formal structure. And it was not uncommon for them to engage in rumbles with other female groups. Girl gang-related groups were more common during the forties than in the sixties, when such groups were almost non-existent. Black street gangs of the sixties did, however, involve girls in many of their criminal acts as lookouts, shoplifters and concealers of weapons and contraband.

The main rivals to the Deacons were the Destroyers, who lived north of Ida B. Wells, and the 13 Cats, who occupied the area south of Oakwood Boulevard to 43rd Street. These groups maintained a fierce rivalry for over 10 years. On the Westside, the Imperial Chaplins and the Clovers were developing a similar rivalry.

Despite these inter-gang rivalries, the violence was minimal compared to the type of violence exemplified by the street gangs of the sixties. While earlier Black street gangs would settle their disputes with zip guns, knives, baseball bats and brass knuckles, the gangs of the sixties employed more lethal weapons. Of course, there were gang killings during the forties and gang members were not immune from engaging in other criminal acts. Such acts as muggings, hold-ups, assaults and burglaries kept many gang members in and out of the juvenile court. Whereas Black youth were once a minority, they now constituted a disproportionate number of the youth population detained in the various youth correctional institutions.

The number of Black juvenile offenders steadily increased and by the early fifties Blacks comprised the largest ethnic group in the juvenile justice system. Although it does not always hold true, I am suggesting that the increase in Black juvenile delinquents can also serve as a social barometer for estimating the rise in Black street gangs. That is to say, delinquents, most likely, are more prone to having gang affiliations than non-delinquents. Despite the increase in criminal activities during the fifties, Black street gangs, as a rule, still maintained some respect for the Black community. Nevertheless, it was becoming apparent that this respect was eroding and being replaced by behavior that diametrically opposed community norms and sanctions. Indeed, the fifties had spawned a generation of Black youth who seemed to thrive on callous behavior, disrespect for adults and senseless violence.

The irony of this dramatic transformation is that it was happening at the time when the Civil Rights Movement was advocating non-violence, racial pride and unity. Even more ironic is the fact that the impetus for the Civil Rights Movement was being generated by other Black youth who realized Black fratricide was no substitute for Black pride. But Black students who were having non-violent demonstrations in the South had little influence on Black street gang members in Chicago who were having their own distinctly more violent demonstrations.

Social service agencies were stymied in the efforts to redirect gang members. The traditional programs they administered failed to meet the needs of troubled youth. As a result, some social agencies initiated non-traditional programs to service gang members. The strategy they used was to employ street workers or outreach workers to work directly with gang members in the streets. This strategy was first used in New York in its Mobilization for Youth Programs and had achieved some mild success. To some degree, this strategy was also successful in Chicago, but the resources available were minimal in comparison to the magnitude of the street gang problem.

In 1956, the YMCA of Metropolitan Chicago initiated its Youth Gang Programs, designed to provide "detached workers" to work with known street gangs. Armed with only a station wagon, a modest expense account and his own human relations skills, the street worker ventured out into the streets to intervene in a process of gang development that had already become firmly entrenched in many communities. At the beginning, this approach was somewhat successful in curbing certain types of delinquent activity, mainly that of gang conflict. But even the most able street worker was not successful in reaching the older hard-core delinquent. The worker soon learned that providing understanding counseling was not enough. He also had to provide gang members opportunities for achievement, which the worker had no power to produce. Early Doty, a former executive director of Youth action, describes this dilemma which weakened the effectiveness of many workers.

> For approximately five years following the advent of street work in 1956, one of the worker's basic tools in affecting upward mobility for ghetto youth was a "job." While this proved to be a valuable tool, it was generally carried forth by a "seat of the pants" approach. There was an absence of sophistication and any clearly refined system was lacking.
>
> A worker was left to develop his own "bag of resources" and expended a great deal of energy and time in dragging youth

from one employer to another. When a job was obtained, it was usually temporary and exploitative in nature.[7]

Later a massive street worker program called STREETS emerged when three other agencies, the Chicago Boys Clubs, Chicago Youth Centers and Hull House Association, saw the need to coordinate their efforts. In 1967, this program was centralized under one agency called Youth Action, which was able to expand its services with the acquisition of federal funds. Still, the problem of gangs persisted and gang activity accelerated. Whereas gang involvement had formerly been seen as an inescapable stage in the lives of most ghetto colony youth, gangs had now achieved greater sophistication and it became advantageous for young adults to remain in their ranks.

Although many street workers performed their duties with great enthusiasm and dedication, their efforts were thwarted by the lack of cooperation from big business and other formal institutions in opening their doors to gang members. The business and political barons of Chicago were simply concerned with pacifying the activities of street gangs and not with providing their members with opportunities that would enable them to escape their world of oppression. And the street worker became the buffer agent by which this could be accomplished. Despite the large amount of funds allocated to street work programs, the Black street gang problem grew to even greater proportions.

As Black street gangs grew larger and more violent, it became increasingly difficult for street workers to maintain their limited influence over gang members. Then, too, there were accounts of some street workers over-identifying with the gangs, thereby neutralizing their ability to rationally assist gang members in changing their ways. Also, the political climate in Chicago was far from conducive to rehabilitating gang members. Cooperation between social agencies and law enforcement agencies left much to be desired, and both agencies accused each other of being responsible for the cleavage. On the one hand, social service agencies were accused of being overly paternalistic, while, on the other hand, law enforcement agencies were accused of being too punitive. Gang members were the victims of their dilemma because neither agency was able to help them adjust to the realities of being oppressed and black in a racist society. Consequently, gang members had little trust in either agency and established their own standards for coping with an environment that appeared to them to be either apathetic or hostile to their needs.

By the early sixties Chicago's Black street gangs had grown to such proportions that they not only posed a threat to themselves but to the Black community as well. The fuse was now burning at a pace so rapid that it was only a matter of time for it to detonate an explosion which would leave the Black community in a state of utter confusion and turmoil. No longer were gang members perceived as misguided youth who were merely going through the pains of adolescence. Now they were being perceived as predators who preyed on whomever they felt infringed on their lust for power. These predatory gangs were not content to emulate their predecessors. Instead, they turned to more criminal activities, and the control of turf became their number one priority. By controlling turf, gangs were able to exercise their muscles to extort monies from businesses and intimidate the Black community. Later, as these gangs became more powerful, many began to engage in the trafficking of drugs.

The recruitment of new members became the means by which gangs could expand their base of power. Whereas membership in Black street gangs had once been mostly voluntary it was now being forced upon non-gang members. The more powerful a gang was, the more difficult it became for non-gang members to resist recruitment. Those who did try to resist were placed in confrontational situations which usually resulted in them being subjected to intimidation, threats or bodily harm. Many youth had no alternative but to join a gang lest they be victimized by it. In fact, in some communities, it got to a point where being a gang member was the safest thing to do.

As gangs became stronger and more common, they began to appeal to non-gang members to join of their own volition. Being a gang member had become a status symbol, and for many alienated Black youths this was extremely important. For many, it provided for the first time a sense of belonging, self esteem and identity. When these needs are juxtaposed to the political climate of the sixties, one can begin to understand their importance. The sixties were a period when most youth, regardless of their racial or economic background, were striving to be recognized on their own terms. Youth movements were common across the nation, and it became apparent that young people no longer held the status quo as being an infallible norm for regulating their lives. Youth of the sixties wanted to become more involved in the political process and were willing to challenge traditional institutions in their newly discovered independence. Because of their unconventional lifestyles, these groups were viewed by the larger society as deviant minorities. Among these groups were the hippies, yippies, Black Panthers, US and SNCC. Although their goals were often different, the quest for social change was common to all. Despite their lack of political awareness, Black street gangs were expressing their own disenchantment in the only way they knew.

Contributing to the expansion of Black street gangs in the sixties was the massive breakdown in major institutions. This collapse was so severe that institutions mandated to serve youth were conspicuously ineffective. For example, the Chicago public schools were more successful in literally pushing more Black youth out into the streets than they were in preparing them to achieve fundamental and essential academic skills. The crisis in the public school began in the fifties when there was a sharp increase in Black student enrollment. Concomitant to this escalation was the dramatic decline in white student enrollment. From every indication, the quality of education in public schools was directly influenced by this transformation. School drop-out rates in some Black communities were as high as 40 percent, leaving many Black youth with nothing to do but waste their idle time in the streets. Then, too, even those Black students who remained in school were subjected to an apathetic educational environment. As a result, the public schools became a primary source for gang recruitment and turf identification. Schools in the sixties became incubators for the breeding of street gangs, even if they were not directly responsible for this development.

Other major institutions such as the Department of Children and Family Services and the Juvenile Court were equally negligent in serving the needs of Black youth. Both of these institutions were disproportionately represented with cases involving Black youth, and both did very little to help Blacks make the types of social adjustments needed to successfully cope with the inequities in their environment. Thus, it should not have been a surprise that many Black youth felt alienated and found the street gang to be the one group they believed was sensitive to their needs. Although their perception may have been incorrect, the street gang was there to accept them as they were. And accept them it did! For those Black youth who had been turned out of school, exposed to the juvenile justice system and who seemed to have no one to help them, the gang was there to boost their lagging self esteem. Now, for the first time, many of these alienated youth could feel wanted and important. The street gang gave them a sense of identity and belonging they never had before. It didn't matter if they were subjected to strict regimentation and had to engage in criminal acts to prove their loyalty. They were willing to take the risk because the gang was the one group that accepted them as they were.

The first blast of the Black street gang explosion had occurred. For ten years, approximately from 1965 to 1975, Black street gangs were to inflict a wound on the Black community that has yet to heal. A pattern of gang behavior had developed which was diametrically in conflict with traditional mores in the Black community. Standards which had previously been honored by Black youth were being completely discarded by Black street gang members who began to establish their own rules of conduct.

On the Southside, the Blackstone Rangers were now the Mighty P. Stone Nation; the Devil Disciples changed to the Black Disciples;

and the Vice Lords now prefixed their name with Conservative. But the Egyptian Cobras, once the Vice Lords, arch rival, had lost much of their power and disintegrated into a number of splinter groups. These groups controlled the vast majority of Black gang members in Chicago, and they were determined to maintain their lofty position, regardless of whom they exploited or victimized.

Of these gangs, however, the Mighty P. Stone Nation achieved the greatest notoriety. In fact, the Mighty P. Stone Nation was probably the largest street gang in the nation, and its reputation received celebrity status. At one time, some of its members toured the country in a production called "Opportunity Knocks" that was conceived and directed by Oscar Brown, Jr; and Sammy Davis, Jr. performed a fund raiser in their behalf. Also, Jeff Fort, the "chief" of the Mighty P. Stone Nation, and Mickey Cogwell were invited by the White House to attend the inauguration of President Richard Nixon in 1968. It has been alleged that the invitation was made to reciprocate for the Mighty P. Stone Nation's role in trying to persuade Blacks to vote for Nixon. Although this allegation was never formally substantiated, the Mighty P. Stone Nation was wooed by many special interest groups. Many of these special interest groups consisted of white liberals who saw the Mighty P. Stone Nation as a means to propagate their own beliefs.

These white liberals were awed by the potential political power of the Mighty P. Stone Nation, and they attempted to translate this power into constructive activities. While this in itself was noteworthy, the romantic image many had of the street gang made it difficult for them to realize the magnitude and complexity of the problem. As a result, the support they gave was often self-serving, contradictory and short-lived. Rarely did they consult with Blacks who had been working with Black street gangs.

While Chicago claimed some of the most notorious Black street gangs, other cities such as Los Angeles, Philadelphia, Newark, Detroit and New York were being beseiged by similar gang problems. Many of these gangs interacted with each other, and in 1967 a meeting was held of major gang leaders. The meeting took place in Resurrection City in Washington, D.C., a site erected as a gathering place for civil rights groups. The outcome of this meeting was not made public, but shortly afterward a national coalition of street gangs was organized and supported with government funds. Leaders from Chicago's Black gangs played a prominent role in this development.

The sixties continued to be a turbulent period for Black street gangs in Chicago. They continued to increase in size as well as in violence. Nothing seemed to suppress their growth or contain their violence—not well-intentioned community organizations, social service agencies, white liberals or even the police.

In 1968, a last-ditch effort was made to rehabilitate Black street gangs. Funds from private foundations and government agencies began to trickle into the hands of a few street gang organizations. Previously these funds had been given to community organizations who, in turn, were supposed to turn them into viable programs to help street gangs secure jobs for their members. But when this arrangement failed to achieve its goal, gang members were then asked to participate along with these organizations to develop more productive programs. One of these programs was Operation Bootstrap, which was designed to create economic opportunities for street gangs. The history of Operation Bootstrap was a short and unsuccessful one. The reason for its failure were many, and during its brief existence charges of mismanagement of funds, unfulfilled promises, political patronage and plain fraud were echoed by both the street gangs and participating agencies. As one gang member put it, "They gave us a strap, but not a boot for it to go on."

In North Lawndale, the Cobras received some assistance in setting up a gasoline station and car wash service. But this undertaking was short-lived. Due to inadequate facilities, insufficient funds, and the lack of proper management, the business lasted less than six months. Later, the Cobras managed a paper factory which was far more successful. But this venture ended in disaster when the building burned down as the result of a fire, which some people believe was the work of an arsonist.

What really happened to the small business ventures of the few street gangs that had begun to achieve some economic stability? First, I would suspect that they lacked sufficient on-going funds to have any long-term success. Second, they lacked sincere professional guidance which could have helped to assure better management. And third, the internal struggle for power between gang members, coupled with the gang mentality, undermined the few chances these groups had to achieve even a small degree of economic security.

As the financial resources of Black street gangs dwindled, so did their influence. Older gang members realized they needed funds to maintain their operations and provide jobs for members. Also, many were becoming tired of constantly fighting each other and were receptive to gaining meaningful and legitimate jobs. The opportunity did come for some in the form of the Chicago Plan, a program designed to obtain jobs for minorities in the building and trade unions. But these unions, true to their traditions, were not supportive of the Plan and resisted its implementation. Under the leadership of the Coalition for United Community Action (CUCA), Black street gangs were mobilized to stop work at construction sites to dramatize the racist policies of the building and trade unions. After a series of fracases, violent demonstrations and political sabotage, the Chicago Plan faltered.

It is noteworthy that during these CUCA demonstrations, particularly the one that tried to shut down the construction site at the University of Illinois Chicago Campus, several gang leaders were arrested. These arrests were followed by many more, and by the early seventies almost all of the major leaders of Black street gangs were incarcerated. The indictments that led to their incarceration ranged from weapons charges and racketeering to murder. Gang leaders claimed they were being convicted on trumped up charges and accused Black organizations of not coming to their defense. Furthermore, they claimed that some Black organizations had abandoned them when they no longer served their vested interests. There was some truth to these allegations because many Black organizations did sever their ties with Black street gangs after the abortive Chicago Plan. Previously, these organizations had been ambivalent about their involvement with Black street gangs. On one hand, they tried to redirect Black street gangs to engage in positive activities. On the other hand, many felt they were losing in their efforts to rehabilitate Black street gangs and thought it would be best to abolish them.

Now that many Black street gangs were without their key leaders, there was a noticeable lull in violent gang activity, especially gang-related killings. This decline is substantiated by the Chicago Police Department records that show 197 gang-related killings from 1972 to 1978 compared to 365 gang-related killings from 1979 to 1983. Although these statistics are not reported by race, it is reasonable to conclude that many resulted from Black street gangs.

As I indicated earlier, gang activity shifted from the streets to the prisons during the seventies. While in prison, many gangs formed coalitions, the two dominant ones being the Folks and the People. Both groups have been transferred to the streets and account for the major confrontations between gangs which have taken place in the eighties. Under coalitions, gang conflicts are far more serious because they involve multiple gangs. This also explains why there are more interracial street gangs today, particularly among Blacks and Hispanics.

The fuse that was ignited in the sixties has been lit again in the eighties. We failed in our efforts to have a positive impact on Black street gangs in the fifties and sixties. The Black street gangs of today are a result of this failure. History should have taught us by now that unsolved problems only perpetuate themselves, usually with greater alarm and intensity. Today's Black street gangs are more volatile, more destructive and more criminally-oriented than their predecessors. They are also better organized to enact these negative traits. Due to the saturation of drugs in the Black community, Black street gangs have organized a network of drug trafficking that generates high profits which they are not willing to relinquish. And, because of the hopelessness and despair that fester in the Black community, they have more than a sufficient number of consumers to support this lucrative enterprise. When people have little hope and are immersed in despair, drugs become a highly marketable product. Contrary to what occurred in New York during the sixties, when Black street gangs became the victims of drugs, Chicago Black street gangs have become the victimizers. That is to say that there is not a large percentage of Black street gangs who are hooked on this poison. Black street gangs have no use for drug addicts because they are often unmanageable and unpredictable.

The death of Ben Wilson did sound an alarm that has sparked a new concern to confront the Black street-gang problem. But the bomb has already been detonated, and we have yet to develop the resources to prevent its destruction from becoming even more devastating.

In summary, I have listed the following factors that have contributed to the development and expansion of Chicago's Black street gangs.

Factors Contributing To the Historical Development of Chicago's Black Street Gangs

1900 - 1930

1. Large migration of Blacks who came to Chicago during the early 1900s, the 20s and the 30s and were confined to underdeveloped segregated areas, thereby compounding the problems of overcrowdedness, unemployment and substandard living conditions.

2. Gradual breakdown of traditional values and mores in the Black community that were the cornerstones for the socialization of Black youth.

3. The Race Riot of 1919 that ignited many young Black males to band together to confront the white hoodlums who were terrorizing the Black community.

4. The failure of city and private agencies to meet the needs of Black families and youth.

5. Acute unemployment among young Black males, resulting in large numbers of them spending idle time in the street for the lack of anything constructive to do.

1930 - 1940

1. The crippling economic impact of the Great Depression on the Black community that escalated the acute unemployment among young Black males and the problems associated with their idleness.

2. A sharp increase in the number of Black delinquents committed to correctional institutions. This is an important factor to note because many of the Black street gangs during this period were first organized at some of these institutions (e.g., St. Charles and Sheridan).

3. The continued breakdown of the Black community's traditional values and mores for socializing Black youth.

1940 - 1950

1. The ineffectiveness of the Juvenile Justice System to prevent the organizing of street gangs within their juvenile corrections institutions. As I have already indicated, many gangs were formed at these institutions. After gangs were organized, recruitment of new members became prevalent at these institutions. To some extent, this trend continues today.

2. The continued failure of major state institutions, city and private agencies, to meet the needs of Black families and youth.

3. Early signs of erosion in the Chicago Public Schools.

1950 - 1970

1. Increasing signs of erosion in the Chicago Public Schools that resulted in the following:
    a. high drop-out rate among Black students
    b. low academic achievement among many Black students
    c. increased violence in the schools
    d. poor supervision of students
    e. breakdown in school discipline
    f. lack of an effective truancy program

2. High unemployment among Black youth.

3. Continued breakdown of traditional community values and mores to socialize Black youth.

4. The deterioration and poor management of Chicago Public Housing.

5. Ambivalence of the Chicago civil rights movement toward Black street gangs. This ambivalence sent mixed signals to Black street gangs, and Black leaders did not take full advantage of the positive elements which many Black street gangs displayed.

6. The failure of social service outreach programs to provide Black gang members with sufficient alternatives and resources to deter them from wanting to remain in gangs. Also, the naiveté of some outreach workers who served as apologists for gangs only obscured some of the violent activities of these gangs.

7. Early signs of drug trafficking by some Black street gangs.

8. The patronizing support of some wealthy while liberals who failed to understand the cultural dynamics associated with Black street gangs, thereby doing more harm than good.

9. The failure of Black leaders to agree on strategies to deal with Black street gangs. This failure was obvious to many gang leaders who exploited it for their own vested interests.

1970 - Present

1. Increased flow of drugs in the Black Community.

2. Increased high unemployment among teenagers and young adults.

3. The lack of viable gang prevention programs to take advantage of the lull in violent gang activity.

4. The early release program of the Department of Corrections that sent older gang members back to the Black community without forewarning or preparing the Black community.

5. The restructuring of street gangs in prison by gang leaders to be more sophisticated, organized and violent.

6. The proliferation of drugs in the Black community resulting in gangs becoming more violent in their quest to control the drug traffic.

II

DEFINITIONS AND THEORIES: THEIR APPLICATION TO BLACK STREET GANGS

IN THE PREVIOUS CHAPTER, I ATTEMPTED TO SUMMARize the development of Chicago's Black street gangs from 1900 to the present, emphasizing many of the key factors which have contributed to their formation and growth. These factors were important to identify because they help us to better understand the historical and social conditions which have influenced this development. However, to fully appreciate the dynamics of Chicago's Black street gangs, there are certain terms and theories which merit examination. First, it will be helpful to discuss a few terms which are commonly associated with youth gangs.

Gang

In the generic sense, the word *gang* is not in itself negative, although most people interpret it as being so. However, the word gang is as American as apple pie and can be traced to colonial times when the British used it to describe their American adversaries. It was also used to describe the bands of rebel cowboys who terrorized the west. (e.g., Dalton Gang, Jesse James Gang, etc). Other examples of a gang were depicted in the movies about the Bowery Boys and Deadend Kids. These gangs were usually glamorized so viewers could be sympathetic with their members.

Then there was the popular comedy series called "Our Gang" that showcased the shenanigans of preadolescents. Of course, the exploits of professional criminals such as Al Capone, John Dillinger and Pretty Boy Floyd gave the word a notoriety that also included the mafia and other criminal groups.

The word gang has also been used to describe the Boy Scouts as well as many other groups that do not exhibit negative behavior. Webster's New Twentieth Century Dictionary gives the following definition of a gang:

> A number of persons associated together in some way; specifically; (a) a number of workmen or laborers under the supervision of a foreman; or as a gang of hod carriers, a gang of stokers; (b) an organized group of criminals; (c) a squad of convicts at work; (d) a group of children or youths from the same neighborhood bonded together for social reasons.

Of the four, definition (d) is the one most commonly associated with youth gangs, although in recent years more youth gangs have been identified with definition (b). This distinction is being made to show that just because a group is called a gang does not automatically mean it is involved in anti-social or criminal activities.

Delinquent

Because there is a high correlation between delinquents and members of youth gangs, this term is often used outside of its proper context. Webster defines *delinquent* as follows:

> Failing or neglecting to do what duty or law requires; guilty of a fault or misdeed.

The word delinquent, then, is a legal term used to describe a youth 17 and under who has been found guilty of a crime and is made a ward of the state. The Illinois Juvenile Court Act defines a delinquent as "any minor who, prior to his 17th birthday, has violated or attempted to violate, regardless of where the act occurred, any federal or state law or municipal ordinance" (Sec. 702-2). However, when charged with such crimes as murder, rape, armed robbery or deviate sexual assault, a youth 15 and over can be exempted from Sec. 702-2 and prosecuted as an adult in Criminal Court. Also, a youth who commits status offense, can be declared a ward of the court if found to be a Minor Requiring Authoritative Intervention (MRAI). When using these statutes for defining a delinquent, we cannot or should not automatically label a young gang member a delinquent. Although we may assume most young gang members commit delinquent or criminal acts, they cannot legally be called delinquents unless adjudicated as one by the Juvenile Court.

Criminal

The word *criminal* is more explicit and does not lend itself to as many interpretations as does the word delinquent. Webster defines criminal as:

> (1) guilty of a crime; (2) having the nature of a crime that violates a law of morality or well-doing; as, theft is a criminal act; (3) involving or relating to a crime; as, a criminal code

Although the word criminal is more explicit than delinquent, we still must be discreet in assigning it to members of youth gangs. Those gang members, 18 and over, who have been convicted by the courts can be called criminals under this definition. However, we must also be careful in assuming that Black street gangs are, in themselves, criminal just because some of their members have been adjudicated as criminals. Then, too, the term *criminal gang* is often misleading when applied to a gang that is comprised of youth under 17 and adults. While the youth under 17 may have engaged in criminal acts, they are treated as delinquents unless assigned to an adult court. Many of today's Black street gangs are more criminally-oriented than their earlier counterparts. This is why the word criminal is exercised more freely in describing these gangs. Despite the criminal tendencies of some Black street gangs, we should not lump all members together and call them criminals. On the other hand, we should not allow ourselves to be deceived by adult criminals who use younger gang members to divert attention from their criminal acts.

Deviant

The word *deviant* is commonly used to describe the behavior of street gang members although, it is also applied to members from other groups. Webster's Dictionary defines deviant as follows:

> deviating from what is accepted as normal or usual; (and) a person who deviates from accepted standards in his beliefs or behavior.

According to this definition, we may attach this word to many groups or persons. Deviant life styles have become common to this society and no longer carry with them the stigma they once did. During the sixties, the hippies, yippies and some Black militant groups were called deviant minorities. However, when deviant is used to describe Black street gangs, it carries with it some inconsistencies. For example, although most Black street gangs deviate from certain conventional standards, they also subscribe to other conventional standards. This suggests that their deviance may not be "anti" in its real intent, but a reaction to not being able to secure material things which are conventional to most Americans. On the other hand, the yippies and hippies denounced many conventional values and developed a set of their own. In the following discussion on gang theory, additional attention will be given to the word deviant as it relates to street gangs.

Studies and Theories on Street Gangs and Delinquency

One of the earliest theories on Chicago's street gangs was formulated by Henry D. McKay and Clifford R. Shaw around 1940. Prior to this, Clifford Shaw had laid the groundwork for their theory in his article "The Juvenile Delinquent," published in *The Illinois Crime Survey* in 1929. McKay and Shaw wanted to explain why street gangs were more pronounced in some communities than in others. To provide them with an answer, they surveyed the demographics of Chicago communities to ascertain their levels of poverty and disorganization. McKay and Shaw concluded from their studies that youth gangs were more likely to spring from impoverished communities which were also disorganized. From the results of their research, the Chicago Area Project was founded, the first major community-based program to deal specifically with delinquent youth and street gangs. The Chicago Area Project focused on organizing community residents to impact institutions to respond to the needs of troubled youth. A year before the publication of the McKay and Shaw study, Frank Tannenbaum's classic *Crime and the Community* was published. Tannenbaum, a criminologist, held the point of view that the individual was first and foremost a product of his environment. Like McKay and Shaw, he believed the community was primarily responsible for the development of delinquents and criminals. This was a sharp contrast from those social scientists who believed that criminal behavior could best be explained by biological and bio-social theories.

Tannenbaum elaborated that the gang or peer group would become the prevailing influence on a youth's values if the group provided the youth with the gratification he yearned for but did not receive from his family or other institutions.

> Once the gang has been developed, it becomes a serious competitor with other institutions as a controlling factor in the boy's life. The importance of the gang lies in its being the only social world of the boy's own age and, in a sense, of his own creation. All other agencies belong to elders; the gang belongs to the boy. Whether he is a leader or just one of the pack, whether his assigned rank has been won by force or ingenuity or represents a lack of superior force or ingenuity, once that rank is established the child accepts it and abides by the rules for changing it.[8]

In fact, Tannenbaum went so far as to suggest that the gang could be "a substitute for home." Indeed, Tannenbaum was among the first to acknowledge what I have called the "street institution" as having such a profound impact on the socialization of youth.

> Another source of failure of the other agencies within the community to fulfill the demands made upon them for winning the loyalty and cooperation of the child who ultimately becomes delinquent may have no direct relation to the family or to the school, but be the results of the environment. The family may live in such crowded quarters as to force the child into the street to such an extent that street life takes the place of family life. The family may be living in a neighborhood where houses of prostitution are located; where gangsters gather; where there is a great deal of perversion of one sort or another; where street pilfering is a local custom; where there is hostility to the police; where there is race friction and warfare; where the children, without the knowledge of their parents, may find means of employment in illicit ways such as acting as procurers for prostitutes or as messengers and go-betweens for criminals; where they can observe the possession of guns, the taking of dope; where they can hear all sorts of tales and observe practices or be invited to participate in practices, or become conscious of habits and points of view of the family in which they live. And because the family under these conditions may be an inadequate instrument for the purpose of supervising and co-ordinating all the child's activities, the family may lose the battle for the imposition of its own standards just because there was a lack of time, energy, space for the doing of the things that needed to be done or for the provision of the room that the children required for the development of their normal play life.[9]

In later years, the works of McKay, Shaw and Tennenbaum were to influence the thinking of social theoreticians who grappled with the problem of delinquency and the street gangs in the fifties. During this later period, the concept of a gang subculture emerged as the prominent theory to explain the development of street gangs. The gang subculture theory was popularized by Albert K. Cohen who wanted to explain why youth who have similar problems come together and develop their own group values which are often in conflict with the values of their community. In *Delinquent Boys: The Culture of the Gang*, Cohen documents a number of street gangs that function according to this theory. Cohen also believed that the working class youth who had middle class values and who did poorly in school were most likely to become a member of a gang subculture. The matrix for Cohen's supposition is presented below.[9]

Working-class socialization + Middle class values of success	Lower-class failure in school system (among many)	Loss of self-esteem and increased feelings of rejection
School dropout and association with delinquent peers (among some)	Increased hostility and resentment toward middle-class standards and symbols, thus reaction formation	Improved self-esteem in a gang context and through negative and malicious delinquent behavior

Another advocate of the delinquent subculture theory is Walter B. Miller. For the most part, Miller supported Cohen's basic premise but added two assumptions of his own: (1) that clear-cut lower-class focal concerns or values exist, independent of other values; and (2) that female-dominated households constitute an integral feature of lower class life-styles and, as such, represent a primary reason for the emergence of street-corner male adolescent groups in lower-class neighborhoods.

Miller's first assumption suggests that a gang subculture, although a part of a larger culture, can be definitely distinguished by its own set of values. His second assumption also appears to be empirically accurate and rather prominently evidenced among Black street gangs.

Cohen and Miller's theories on delinquent subculture were to be further developed by Robert K. Merton, who spoke of social structure and anomie as being the crucial factors in shaping delinquent/deviant behavior. (The groundwork for Merton's thesis was laid by Emile Durkheim's seminal work, "Suicide.") Merton indicated that behavior was a reaction or response to an institution or social norm. The type of behavior exhibited by a person, then, depended on how responsive the institution or social norm was to a particular need. Merton then identified five modes of adaptation which are used in response to cultural goals and institutionalized means.

Modes of Adaptation	Cultural Goals	Institutionalized Means
I Conformity	+	+
II Innovation	+	—
III Ritualism	—	+
IV Retreatism	—	—
V Rebellion	+/—	+/—

Note: + = acceptance; — = rejection; +/— = rejection of prevailing values and substitution of new values.

If we are to accept Merton's five modes of adaptation without any reservation, then it would be safe to assume that Black street gangs are rebellious in their response to institutions and social norms. However, we must be careful in making such a distinction because rarely are theories demonstrated in reality in their purest interpretation. On the other hand, if we feel Merton's theory has validity, we can assume that it is applicable to some members of Black street gangs. Richard A. Cloward and Lloyd E. Ohlin expounded on the delinquent subculture theory in their book *Delinquency and Opportunity*. Although they supported this theory in principle, Cloward and Ohlin also believed there existed a differential opportunity structure for disadvantaged youth that caused poor self-concepts and frustrations. As a result, these youth would use illegitimate means to achieve success through one of the three gang types shown in the following diagram:

Limited access to legitimate means of achieving desired economic success	Feeling of frustration and deprivation, leading to gang formation
	Stable, integrated conventional and criminal systems = criminal, theft gang
Predominance of one of three types of gangs, depending on the integration of conventional adult value and behavior systems in a neighborhood	Non-integrated systems, absence of criminal organization, instability = conflict, violent gangs
	In either type of neighborhood, double failure, residual adolescents = retreatist "gang" or, more accurately, retreatist response

Obviously, Cloward and Ohlin's gang types cannot be taken literally as models for contemporary Black street gangs because they are too rigid in their definition. However, when considered collectively, we can discern some of the characteristics of Black street gangs and, therefore, use them as a general overview of how some street gangs are formed.

What all of these theories fail to delineate is the impact of institutional racism on Black street gangs. Instead, they lump all street gangs under the same categories, as though racial distinction has nothing to do with why and how some Black street gangs develop. This is a disservice to Black street gangs. Although there are universal characteristics that can be applied to most street gangs, Black street gangs are unique. I contend that if we are to fully understand and appreciate the dynamics of Black street gangs, we must view them from a social and historical perspective; and from this perspective, the taint of racism is abundantly evident. To ignore this fact is to pretend that Black people have never been oppressed in this country and are assured the freedoms and privileges enjoyed by whites. Of course, this is ridiculous and any sensible person knows there is not one part of the Black Experience that has been free from institutional racism. This is particularly true in the case of most Black youth who live in communities where few institutions are responsive to their exceptional needs.

One reason why racism has been omitted from most theories on youth gangs is that the overwhelming majority of the theoreticians have been white. White social scientists have historically been cautious in identifying racism as a major cause for the social inequities experienced by Black people. Although they will avidly declare poverty as a factor contributing to these inequities, rarely will they identify racism in the same context. Yet, the blocked opportunities which Cloward and Ohlin speak about and the "differential accessibility" described by Merton are, at least from my vantage point, the results of racism. My concern over the fact that racism has been flagrantly ignored in most theories on street gangs is not to make excuses for the violent activities of Chicago Black street gangs. As debilitating as racism is, I do not approve of

Black-on-Black crime as a response to it. And Black street gang violence is essentially Black-on-Black crime. However, I also feel we cannot sweep racism under the carpet and pretend it doesn't exist.

To what degree racism impacts Black street gang development, I cannot honestly say. But we do know (or should know) that the positive socialization of Black youth is impaired when they are raised in what Dr. Leon Chestang, a Black psychologist, describes as a hostile environment.

> Three conditions, socially determined and institutionally supported, characterize the black experience: social injustice, societal inconsistency, and personal impotence. To function in the face of any one of them does cruel and unusual violence to the personality. To function in the face of all three subjects the personality to severe crippling or even destruction. These three crucial conditions, however, confront the black person throughout his life, and they determine his character development.[10]

As a result of these conditions, Black youth develop one of the following types of behavior:

1. **Adaptive Behavior** — accept status in life and try to make the most of it;
2. **Modified Behavior** — Modify values to be more acceptable to whites; or
3. **Compensated Behavior** — Engage in destructive activities to compensate for oppressed status.

As one would expect, under these conditions, many Black youth develop compensated behavior that nullifies their chances of achieving their true potential. So long as the exceptional needs of Black youth are not being met by the family or other institutions, the street gang will continue to be an alternative for them. In the following chapter, I will discuss reasons why the street gang is appealing to some Black youth.

III

WHEN INSTITUTIONS FAIL, THE GANG WILL PREVAIL: WHY GANGS HAVE APPEAL

REGARDLESS OF THE RISKS ASSOCIATED WITH BEING A member of a gang, Black street gangs do have appeal for many Black youth. Even though some youth become members of street gangs due to forced recruitment, there are large numbers who join willingly. Also, we know that some youth who are forced to join gangs often enjoy being a gang member after they have been indoctrinated. What makes the gang attractive to some youth? Why does the gang have a mesmerizing effect on them? Why is the gang one of the few institutions in the Black community that is relevant to some youth? Why are some youth willing to risk their lives for the gang? In the two previous chapters, these questions were briefly discussed. This chapter will elaborate on these questions by identifying five factors which make street gangs appealing to youths:

1. Sense of Identity
2. Sense of Belonging
3. Sense of Power
4. Sense of Security
5. Sense of Discipline

1. **Sense of Identity**

When Black street gang members boldly shout out the name of their gang, they are letting everybody know who they identify with. They are, in fact, expressing a sense of identity. Aside from their racial identity, most people like to be identified with the profession, fraternity, team or social club with which they are primarily associated. Without this sense of identity, individuals are grouped with the masses, receiving no special recognition. For some people this presents no problem, but for Black youth who have low self-esteem, identifying with a group is extremely important. The gang provides a youth with a name to which he can attach himself. It gives him a sense of recognition. Because most Black street gang members have not received this type of recognition in their homes or from other institution, they take pride in their gang name. This pride is scribbled on buildings (graffiti) and showcased wherever possible to let the community know who they are. Being members of street gangs provides these youth an opportunity to compensate for low self-esteem. It allows them to feel, probably for the first time in their lives, that they are, indeed, somebody.

2. **Sense of Belonging**

Most people desire to belong to something. It is a universal feeling that transcends race, class, or gender. This feeling of belonging becomes even more important when people feel unwanted and alienated. When this feeling does occur, some people are willing to do almost anything to be accepted. They are even willing to give up some of their individual freedoms to become a member of a group. And when the group consists of other members who have also been alienated, they find even greater satisfaction. There is nothing more self-gratifying than to be accepted by others who can identify with your problems. The axiom "birds of a feather flock together" exemplifies this acceptance. To share common values and needs is rewarding. This is why fraternities are so popular among many college youth, and why people join professional organizations, social clubs, etc. Another example of this type of fraternalism can be seen among athletic teams.

The point I am trying to make is that the street gang provides many Black youth this same sense of belonging. When a youth becomes a member of a street gang, he immediately finds himself associating with youth who have similar needs and values. He gains satisfaction in being recognized as a member (sense of identity) and is made to feel important. Despite its restrictions and punitive measures, belonging to a street gang does allow him to feel good about himself. Now he belongs to something that provides him identity, status and power. These are major incentives and I can think of no other group or institution in the Black community that provides a youth with these things. Also, the loyalty and comradeship among gang members are as strong, if not stronger, than in most traditional groups, i.e. fraternities, unions, social clubs, etc.

3. Sense of Power

Throughout the history of man, power has always been an important factor in determining the outcome of events. As a result, most people are obsessed with power and those who have it flaunt it around as though they were kings and queens. Conversely, those who do not have power are constantly struggling to obtain it.

It is little wonder, then, that many Black youth become inflicted with the "power syndrome." And why shouldn't they when they are constantly being exposed to it in the movies, on television and the various other media. Indeed, they are programmed to feel if you want something in this world, you must have some power. Those without power generally find themselves being exploited by those who have power. It has been like this since the beginning of man.

For Black youth who are alienated and who have low self esteems, having a sense of power is extremely important. It provides them, at least, with a feeling of being somebody and of having some control over their lives. It also serves as a shield to help them feint off threatening situations. Belonging to a gang provides a youth with a "sense of security" and a reputation that illicits fear and/or respect from his peers. The gang becomes his base of power and allows him to feel important in a society where he would otherwise be, almost, completely ignored.

To be sure, the "sense of power" Black street gangs provide their members is not imaginary. As power brokers in their communities, Black street gangs are highly visible. In some communities, their mere presence provoke fear among the residents. And their criminal activities only escalate the paranoid that many residents constantly live with.

However, for many alienated Black youth, having a "sense of power" is something they feel is crucial to their survival.

4. Sense of Security

Despite its many hazards, the gang does provide a youth with a sense of security. For those youths who feel insecure and alienated, membership in a gang especially helps to ameliorate these feelings. When a youth must grow up in a high-risk community, it is to his advantage to belong to some group that can provide him protection. Ideally, this protection should be provided by the family. But, for many reasons, some families cannot adequately perform this critical function. As a result, the gang becomes the family for many youth. If not the gang—who else? Rarely does a Black youth receive a sense of security from other institutions. All too often Black youth are left on their own to survive the best way they can. Under these circumstances, there is little wonder many Black youths are drawn to the gang.

5. Sense of Discipline

Contrary to popular opinion, Black youth do respond to discipline. In fact, it is the lack of discipline many receive that contributes to their cantankerous behavior. But discipline for Black youth must be firm and consistent. To be effective, it cannot be erratic and patronizing as it is generally practiced by most institutions.

The Black street gang, with its rigid hierarchy and system of punishment and rewards, provides a youth with a highly disciplined structure. It is a structure that tells him what to do, how to do it, and why he should do it. Discipline among gang members is critical to a gang's reputation, prestige and survival. Many Black gangs are organized like para-military groups to ensure the tightest control over their members. They not only indoctrinate their members, but infuse in them a sense of loyalty and obedience that are binding on their behavior for life. This explains why some gang members will do almost anything for the gang. They are totally committed to it and are willing to relinquish their personal egos in the interest of the gang.

The five factors I have identified can also be interpreted as needs. These are needs most people have, and the absence of any one can leave a void in the social and emotional development of an individual. To appreciate the importance of these needs, we must only to relate them to A.H. Maslow's classic theory on the Hierarchy of Basic Needs. Maslow's theory sought to explain what motivates individuals and to establish why individuals' drives vary in relationship to their fulfillment of specific needs. From his many studies and the works of other functionalist social scientists, Maslow identified five basic needs in his hierarchy:

1. Physiological Needs
2. Safety Needs
3. Belongingness and Love Needs
4. Esteem Needs
5. Need for Self-Actualization

By interfacing the factors I have identified with Maslow's hierarchy of needs, we can better appreciate why the Black street gang has appeal to some Black youth. The following schematic illustrates this juxtaposition:

Schematic For Juxtaposing Factors That Influence Black Gang Members and Maslow's Hierarchy of Needs

Physiological Needs	Safety Needs	Belonginess and Love Needs	Esteem Needs	Self-Actualizing
- Security - Power	- Security - Power	- Identity - Belonging - Discipline	- Identity - Belonging - Power	(It is highly questionable whether or not Black Street Gangs can ever help their members achieve this.)
(Some Black Street Gangs do provide their members with life-giving resources, e.g. housing, food, clothes.)				

The interfacing of Maslow's hierarchy of needs and the needs of some Black youth is not intended to be food for intellectual discourse. Rather, it is my attempt to explain, in part, why the street gang has appeal for some Black youth. Ideally, these needs would be met by the family or other institutions in the Black community. Unfortunately, this is not the case for many Black youth and, as a result, the street gang becomes their greatest ally. For some Black youth the street gang takes the place of their family. Of course, we do not like to admit this fact.

To suggest that street gangs are necessary because they do meet some basic needs of Black youth reflects a serious breakdown in our institutions. But until we are successful in reinforcing those strengths which still exist among most Black families and in holding institutions accountable for their services to youth, the Black street gang will continue to prevail. It is a fact we really need not debate because self-preservation will always be the highest priority for Black youth who live in an environment that does not fulfill their basic needs.

IV

MYTHS, FACTS AND REALITIES ABOUT BLACK STREET GANGS

DESPITE VOLUMINOUS THEORIES ON STREET GANGS, specially funded programs to curb their activities and massive police crackdowns, street gangs still exist and, from every indication, will continue to exist. This, in itself, should not be too alarming, for as I have already indicated, street gangs have been around in some form or another since the founding of America. In fact, we may even take some comfort in saying that youth gangs are as American as apple pie. What makes my prognosis alarming is that, over the years, youth gangs have become more violent and destructive to themselves and to their communities. The youth gangs of today no longer consist of neighborhood peers merely banding together to exercise their independence and act out their adolescent frustrations. To some extent, the youth gangs of the past were tolerated because we could blame their behavior on poor environments, broken homes and other social inequities. Yet, these conditions have become inconsequential today—even though they still exist—because of the disruptive impact youth gangs have on their communities. The violence perpetrated by some Black street gangs has made even those who once sympathized with them critical of their activities. Although it is unreasonable to attribute all violence in the Black community to street gangs, violent offenses that are gang related do merit special concern.

There is a high correlation between youth gangs and violence committed by youth. According to the U.S. Department of Justice, one-half of all crimes are committed by youth under age 20. The profile for these youthful offenders reveal that they:

- are predominantly male
- are disproportionately Black and Hispanic
- are economically disadvantaged
- are likely to have interpersonal difficulties and behavorial problems
- are likely to be school drop-outs
- are likely to come from one-parent female headed families
- are likely to be a member of a gang

The increased violence by Chicago Black street gangs is no doubt spurred by the drug traffic. While the Black community has never been immune to drugs, there has been a dramatic increase in drugs since the sixties. This increase has included what was once considered a middle class drug, with the easy accessibility of cocaine and its synthetic companion, crack. These drugs have created an unprecedented demand from all sectors of the Black community. Usually, when the demand for a product is great, there is intense competition for the right to be the supplier. It is not being presumptuous to say that most gang-related crimes in the 80s, especially the killings, have been associated with drugs. The influx of drugs in the Black community has been catastrophic and devastating. Even worse, it has been the catalyst for some Black street gangs to accelerate their criminal and violent acts. As a result, drugs have become the number one priority of many Black street gangs, and the profits generated from this poison serve as an incentive for them to engage in violent acts, if necessary. Although these profits are mostly shared among adult gang members, they also serve as bait to entice younger gang members to be drug runners.

The cycle for Black street gangs appears to be unchanging and unyielding. It is a cycle that will cripple thousands of Black youth. An inordinate number of these youths will most likely become hooked on drugs, incarcerated or killed before they reach their 30th birthdays.

The questions we must address are whether this cycle can ever be broken or whether we can reduce the amount of violence by Black street gangs? My response to the first question is a tentative no. Because street gangs have become so firmly entrenched in most Black communities, I cannot fathom gangs dissolving so long as the Black community remains in a state of poverty, chaos and oppression. My response to the second question is a tentative yes. I have qualified my response because I believe that before we can reduce gang related violence, we must, first, dispel some of the myths we have about street gangs. It has been due to these myths that our efforts to curb gang violence have been minimum at best. Some of the myths we need to dispel are as follows:

Myth 1: That traditional social service agencies can have a significant impact on street gangs.
Fact: There is no substantial empirical evidence to confirm that these agencies have been effective in working with street gangs. Although some of these agencies did impact gangs during the sixties with their detached/outreach worker programs, these programs eventually became ineffective. And now that some Black street gangs are more sophisticated and violent, social service agencies are even less likely to impact street gang members.

Myth 2: That youth workers/social workers can effectively work with gang members aged 19 and over.
Fact: Most older gang members are involved in criminal activities, and it is not practical to expect youth workers/social workers to change their behavior.

Myth 3: That street gangs can be conveniently classified as conflict, criminal or retreatist.
Fact: These are theoretical labels that should only be seen as group responses to situations and not applied categorically to any

one street gang. On different occasions, Black street gangs may identify with all of these labels, although few, if any, would be categorized as retreatist.

Myth 4: That some Black street gangs have memberships over 20,000.

Fact: This was believed to be true of some Black street gangs in the sixties when they called themselves "nations." However, these figures were never substantiated and, no doubt, were exaggerated. Then, too, even if some Black street gangs approximated these membership figures, a large percentage of them were fringe members.

Myth 5: That the hierarchy of some Black street gangs is so rigid, leaders are able to exercise absolute authority over all their members.

Fact: While some Black street gangs are well organized, it is only among core members that the leaders have the greatest influence. This also accounts for the reason truces between rival gangs are usually violated because leaders are not able to control all members.

Myth 6: All street gang members are delinquents.

Fact: While there is a high correlation between delinquents and street gang members, we should not assume that all street gang members are delinquents. As I have indicated, a delinquent is a youth 17 and under who has been made a ward of the Juvenile Court. All youthful gang members do not commit criminal acts and, therefore, some never appear in Juvenile Court.

Myth 7: If Black street gangs did not have forced recruitment, they would eventually disappear.

Fact: Although forced recruitment increases a gang's membership, there are a sufficient number of youth who want to join a gang without being recruited.

Myth 8: That racial considerations are not important when examining Black street gangs. In other words, all street gangs are influenced by universal factors which transcend race.

Fact: This myth permeates the literature on street gangs and does a disservice to Black street gangs. Although there are common characteristics among gangs of all racial groups, Black street gangs have a unique and distinct character. Moreover, this character cannot be fully understood or appreciated by merely lumping Black gangs with other gangs. Quite the contrary, Black street gangs are a part of the Black experience and, therefore, must be examined within the context of slavery, racism, colonialism and economic oppression.

Myth 9: Organized sports are a deterrent to street gangs.
Fact: Black youths who are attracted to street gangs are usually not too athletic and when introduced to sports generally do not perform well. Also, when they do participate, they often compensate for their lack of skill by being overly aggressive.

After correcting some of the myths many people have about Black street gangs, I will identify those realities we must face if we are seriously interested in controlling the development of Black street gangs and reducing the violence that many perpetrate.

Reality 1: The trafficking of drugs in the Black community must be stopped!
Reason: Drugs are largely responsible for most of the violence in the Black community and have become a primary source of income for Black street gangs. Also, the revenues from the sale of drugs distract many Black youth from seeking legitimate employment and serve as bait for them to join gangs.

Reality 2: Public schools must be mandated to ensure every student receives a quality education!
Reason: Youth who achieve in school are less prone to becoming involved with gangs. Also, the drop-out rate among Black youth is extremely high, and school drop-outs are more prone to becoming involved with gangs.

Reality 3: Public housing in its present form must be totally abolished!

Reason: Public housing has become a sanctuary for many Black street gangs. Also, the poor management and poor maintenance of public housing have created a deplorable and chaotic environment that contributes to gang violence.

Reality 4: Year-round, part-time employment must be provided for every "disadvantaged" Black youth between the ages of 16 and 19.

Reason: Youth who have some type of employment are less prone to becoming involved with gangs.

Reality 5: The Juvenile Justice System must be more innovative in dealing with gang recruitment, gang indoctrination and gang harassment among its clients.

Reason: For many Black youth who are adjudicated delinquents, the Juvenile Justice System reinforces their exposure and association to and with gangs.

Reality 6: The Black Church must regain credibility among troubled Black youth and assume a leadership role in dealing with Black street gangs.

Reason: Despite its many shortcomings, the Black Church remains the most viable institution with the resources and leadership to significantly impact Black street gangs.

Reality 7: Black men, professional and non-professional, must organize themselves to become more involved with Black youth.

Reason: A disproportionate number of Black street gang members are from single-parent homes headed by females. Also, Black men have the responsibility for helping Black male youth achieve adulthood. The lack of strong positive guidance from males leads many Black youth to join gangs.

Reality 8: The police, especially youth officers and members of the Gang Crime Section, must work more closely with social agencies, schools and churches to develop better relations with troubled Black youth.

Reason: Improved relations between the police and troubled Black youth would help to reduce the tensions between them which often lead to misunderstandings and premature confrontations.

Reality 9: The Illinois Department of Children and Family Services must improve its services to troubled Black youth.

Reason: This large state agency has a history of not providing troubled Black youth with quality service, thus compounding the problems they already have.

The realities I have identified are not intended to be the solution to the problem of Black street gangs. Such a claim would be irresponsible and misleading. The problem of Black street gangs is complex and imbued with so many unpredictable variables, it will not be resolved easily. Black gangs have become so much a part of their communities that I do not believe we will curb their development in the foreseeable future. Nonetheless, I do believe that much of the violence being perpetrated by Black street gangs can be significantly lowered if we respond to the myths and the realities I have listed.

EPILOGUE

A GENERATION NOT YET BLESSED

THE PROBLEM OF BLACK STREET GANGS IS ONE FOR which the entire Black community must bear some responsibility. Indeed, it is a problem that is a reflection of the Black community's failure to properly supervise its youth. Regardless of the external causes that contribute to this problem, the Black community must be held collectively accountable for the behavior of Black youth. This should not be seen as being unreasonable because it is not as though Black gang members are aliens from another planet. Quite to the contrary, they come from the same Black community where, as children, they once attended Sunday school, played softball in the playground and performed shenanigans in the streets. Yet, now we see many of them as "mercenaries" fearing for our safety when they approach us on the streets; feeling helpless to correct them when they are wrong.

Until the Black community collectively assumes the responsibility that it once did for raising its youth, Black street gangs will continue to unleash their fury and violence. The Black community has abrogated this critical responsibility and no longer provides Black youth with a support system to nurture their development. This is a dramatic departure from the way our grandparents and their parents responded to the challenge of raising children. Despite slavery and other forms of oppression, they somehow managed to instill discipline in Black children and raise them to be respectful toward elders and to respect their community. They understood that if Black people were ever to regain our greatness, Black children had to work harder, be smarter and be stronger than those who were oppressing us. And so in the tradition of our African ancestors, they did everything possible to raise Black children to be disciplined, courteous and responsible.

Today, however, most of these values have been displaced by confusion, contradictions, betrayal and apathy. The Black community has been unable to sustain those values that were the foundation for the socialization of Black youth. As a result, we now have a generation of Black youth who represent two extremes. One extreme is the "Buppies," young Black professionals who have benefited from the civil rights movement but do not always identify with the problems in the Black community. The other extreme constitutes those alienated Black youth, many of whom are members of Black street gangs, who vent their frustration and anger on the Black community. Between these two extremes lie the majority of Black youth who do the best they can to neutralize the negative forces that keep the Black community in a state of chaos and despair. It is fortunate that many Black youth do try to adhere to mores that best serve the interest of the Black community. Were this not the case, the size of some Black street gangs would increase enormously. But we can take little pride in this fact. If conditions do not improve considerably in the Black community, this fact could drastically change. Black street gangs are poised and waiting for more disenchanted and alienated youth to join their ranks. They realize that their strength lies not only in numbers but their ability to perpetuate these numbers over many, many years. Finally, if the Black community does not collectively assume the responsibility for the caring, education and protection of all its youth, the future of Black people is indisputably bleak. I cannot fathom any people achieving greatness if they do not provide their youth with the basic support systems needed for their development. As it stands now, Black street gangs are an obstacle not only to the positive development of their members but, also, to the Black community as well.

FOOTNOTES

1. St. Clair Drake and Horace R. Clayton, *Black Metropolis.* (New York: Harper and Row, 1945), p. 202.
2. Chicago Commission on Race Relations, *The Negro In Chicago*, (Chicago: University of Chicago Press, 1922), p. 12.
3. Allan H. Spear, *Black Chicago: The Making of A Negro Ghetto.* (Chicago: University of Chicago Press, 1967), p. 68.
4. Frederic M. Thrasher, *The Gang*, (Chicago: University of Chicago Press, 1968), p. 132.
5. Ibid., p. 135.
6. Drake and Clayton, op. cit., p. 203.
7. Earl Doty, "New Dimensions of Street Work," *Viewpoint*, (YMCA of Metropolitan Chicago, Third Quarter, 1968), p. 8.
8. Frank Tannenbaum, *Crime and the Community*, (New York: Ginn and Co., 1938), p. 21.
9. Ibid., p. 22.
10. Leon W. Chestang, "Character Development in a Hostile Environment" (Self-published document, 1972), p. 2.

BIBLIOGRAPHY

Home Is A Dirty Street: The Social Oppression of Black Children, Useni Eugene Perkins, Third World Press, Chicago

The Gang, Frederic M. Thrasher, University of Chicago Press, Chicago

The Blackstone Rangers, R.T. Sale, Random House, New York

Street Kids, Larry Cole, Grossman Publishers, New York

Delinquent Boys, Albert K. Cohen, The Free Press, New York

Action On The Streets, Frank Carney, Hans W. Mattick, John D. Callaway, Associated Press, New York

A Nation of Lords, David Dawley, Anchor Books, New York

Youth on the Streets, Saul Bernstein, Associated Press, New York

Delinquency and Opportunity, Richard A. Cloward and Lloyd E. Ohlin, Free Press, Glencoe, Illinois

Theories of Delinquency, Donald Shoemaker, Oxford University Press, New York

Motivation and Personality, A.H. Maslow, Harper & Row Publishers, New York

APPENDIX

Evolution of Chicago's Black Street Gangs 1900 - Present

I. Period of Urbanization 1900 - 1920
   1. Low Gang Activity
   2. Small Groups
   3. Low Frequency of Delinquency
   4. Low Frequency of Criminal Activity
   5. Loosely Organized
   6. Restricted Mobility
   7. Age Range 16-20
   8. Low Inter-Group Conflict
   9. Voluntary Membership
   10. Restricted Territory (Black Belt)

II. Period of Stabilization 1920 - 1930
   1. Moderate Gang Activity
   2. Medium Sized Groups
   3. Increased Frequency of Delinquency
   4. Low Frequency of Criminal Activity
   5. Loosely Organized
   6. Restricted Mobility
   7. Age Range 16-22
   8. Low Inter-Group Conflict
   9. Voluntary Membership
   10. Restricted Territory (Black Belt)

III. Period of Economic Repression 1930 - 1940
   1. Increased Gang Activity
   2. Group Size Increased
   3. High Frequency of Delinquency
   4. Moderate Frequency of Criminal Activity
   5. Better Organized
   6. Increased Mobility
   7. Age Range 14-24
   8. Increased Inter-Group Conflict
   9. Voluntary Membership
   10. Expanded Territory (Black Belt, Near West Side)

IV. Period of Turf Control and Gang Banging 1940 - 1950
   1. High Gang Activity
   2. Large Groups
   3. High Frequency of Delinquency
   4. Increased Frequency of Criminal Activity
   5. Formally Organized
   6. Expanded Mobility
   7. Age Range 12-26
   8. Increased Inter-Group Conflict
   9. Beginning of Forced Membership
   10. Turf Control and Expansion

V. Period of Intensed Gang Conflict & Recruitment 1950 - 1960
   1. Intensed Gang Activity
   2. Large Group Membership
   3. Very High Frequency of Delinquency
   4. High Frequency of Criminal Activity
   5. Highly Organized
   6. Increased Expansion and Mobility
   7. Age Range 10-30
   8. Intensed Inter-Group Conflict
   9. Intensed Recruitment
   10. Intensed Turf Control and Expansion

VI. Period of Increased Expansion and Turbulence 1960 - 1970
   1. Intensed Gang Activity
   2. Large Group Membership - Nations and Group Mergers
   3. Very High Frequency of Delinquency
   4. Very High Frequency of Criminal Activity
   5. Highly Organized
   6. Increased Expansion and Mobility
   7. Age Range 8-35
   8. Intensed Inter-Group Conflict
   9. Intensed Recruitment
   10. Turf Domination & Economic Expansion

VII. Period of Retrenchment 1970 - 1980
   1. Decreased Gang Activity
   2. Disrupted Groups and Decreased Membership
   3. Decreased Frequency of Delinquency

      4. Decreased Frequency of Criminal Activity
      5. Loosely Organized
      6. Disrupted Mobility
      7. Age Range 8-40
      8. Decreased Inter-Group Conflict
      9. Decreased Recruitment
     10. Uprooted Territory

VIII. Period of Retaliation 1980 - Present
      1. Increased Gang Activity
      2. Group Reorganization and Increased Membership
      3. Increased Frequency of Delinquency
      4. Increased Frequency of Criminal Activity
      5. Highly Organized
      6. Controlled Mobility
      7. Age Range 8-50
      8. Moderate Inter-Group Conflict
      9. Increased Recruitment
     10. Reclaiming of Turf and Control of Criminal Activities

Glossary of Street & Gang Terms

Street & Gang Term	Definition
Ace	$1.00 or good fellow
A Fair One	A fair fight between gangs or gang members, fought in accordance with rules
Big Boy	One of the higher-ups
Bit	Jail Term
Blade, Shiv or Shank	Knife
Blanket	Top Coat
Blast	Shoot
Blowman	One picked to shoot gun in a gang fight
Bomb or Lead	Automobile
Bop	To fight
Bopping Club	A fighting gang
Boxed	Close in, surround, rival gang or individual member

Bread, Gold or Loot	Money
Bug	Burglar Alarm
Bugged Joint	Place protected by a burglar alarm
Bust or Busted	A shooting affray between two gangs, an arrest
Cat	Sharp fellow
That Cat	Referring to someone
Cheese	To give police information about a gang member
Cheesy	Traitorous
Chick	A girl
Chicken	Display cowardice
Chippy	A young girl
Chuckers	Dice
Clique	A gang
Cocktail party	To use a molotov cocktale
Cool	An uneasy armistice
Coolie	Non-gang boy
Cool it!	Take it easy!
Copecetic	O.K.
Crazy	Very good
Debs	Girls affiliates of gang boys
Didley bop	First-class gang fighter
Dog it	Get cold feet, turn coward
Doll	A good-looking girl
Doogie	Drugs
Drop a	Give me a
Dude	A gang boy
Dues	Money chipped in for wine
Duke	To fight (with fists)
Eyeball	Look a policeman up and down
Fin	$5.00
Flam or to Jive	To lie
For Real	To be earnest, sincere
Frail	A girl
Gams	Legs
Gig	A party
Glimmer	Black eye
Glom	to grab or steal or a stupid person
Go By	Pas up - snob
Go Down	To attack another gang, to declare war
Grind	Wine

Heart	Courage
Heater	Gun
Homemade	Zip gun
Top or set	A dance
To Be High	To be intoxicated with drugs or alcohol
To Be Hep or Hip	To be wise
A Hipster	One who is smart
Jap	To ambush or attack an individual
Jara	Policeman
La Jara	The cops
Jitterbut	To fight
Jock a Boppin	Sexual intercourse
Jump	Dance
Knife the Scene	Leave, depart
To Play Knock Knock	To knock on the door of a gang enemy and beat him up when he opens the door
Lean	Punch
Lip	Argumentative words
Lineup	Intercourse with one girl by group of males
Make it	Leave
Meet	A meeting, usually of gang chiefs
Packing	Carrying a firearm
Pad	Living quarters
Pad money	Rent
Pegged	A marked fact or enemy
Piece	Weapon usually a gun
To Play the Dozen	To speak disparagingly of another family
A Punk	A boy who won't fight; a boy with no gang affiliation
Punk Out	Display Cowardice
Rank	To insult (usually profanity concerning a boy's mother)
Rap	To talk
Real Gone	Perfect
Rep	Reputation, usually fighting reputation
Rumble	Gang fight
To Score	to win
Set	Party
Shaking	What is happening or about to happen
Shin Battle	Intra-gang practice or test-of-mettle fight among gang members

Shuffle	To engage in a fist fight
Slamus	Jail
Slicker	Smart fellow (chisler type)
Snag	To attack an individual
Sneaky Pete	Cheap wine
Sound	Talk
Square	One who doesn't like gangs
Stash	To hide something
State	Fancy fight steps learned in a correctional institution
Stingy	Short-brimmed hat
Stick Man	Armorer for a gang
Stud	Sharpie
Suicide Squad	Made up of a group of boys who feel they have no future
Swag	Loot
Swing With a Gang	To be a gang member
Teach	Teacher
Thunderbird	Wine
Tight	Friendly as between gangs
To sound	To joke or needle
Turf	A gang's own territory, also street or sidewalk
Turkey	Easy to make, understand
Warlord	Prime minister of gang or one who plans strategy
Wheel of Short	Automobile
A "Win"	When the other size runs away
Zip Gun	A homemade gun capable of firing a .22 caliber bullet, made with a car aerial and a wooden stock or cap pistol frame

Major Chicago Street Gangs

Black Gangster Disciple Nation

Colors: Black and Blue   Racial Make-up 100: Black

Symbols: Crossed pitch forks; 6 pointed star (star of David) Heart with wings; earring in right, hat tilted to right.

Black P Stone

Colors: Red and Black   Racial Make-up: 100: Black

Symbols: Half crescent moon pyramid; earring in left ear, hat tilted to left.

Cobra Stones

Colors: Red and Black   Racial Make-up 100% Black

Symbols: Five pointed star; half crescent moon.

El Rukns

Colors: Blue and Red   Racial Make-up: 100% Black

Symbols: Five point star-pyramid with eye-sword-sun rising behind the pyramid-circle seven.

Useni Eugene Perkins is a poet, playwright and social practitioner whose works have been widely published. He is also the editor of *Black Child Journal*. His social commentary on Black children, *Home Is A Dirty Street*, was cited by Lerone Bennet, Jr., as "...one of the most important books on the sociology of the streets since publication of *Black Metropolis*." Among his many produced plays are *Black Fairy, Image Makers, Professor J.B., Legend of Deadwood Dick, The Murder of Steve Biko* and *The Last Phoenix*.

The father of three children, he is the former executive director of the Better Boys Foundation Family Center in Chicago, and was the recipient of a Chicago Community Trust Fellowship in 1985. Mr. Perkins authored the work *Harvesting New Generations – The Positive Development of Black Youth* in 1986. He is currently employed as Director of the DuSable Museum of African American History in Chicago.